I0421087

# The Politics of the Crucifixion
## By CL Gammon

Text Copyright © 2015 by CL Gammon
All Rights Reserved

Cover Illustration Copyright © 2015 by
Kimberly Gammon, All Rights Reserved

For all those willing to seek after the truth.

## Special Thanks:

The cover illustration is an original, hand drawn image produced by Kimberly Gammon. She gave permission for its use. Thank you, Kimberly.

# Preface

I am a Christian, but I do not make any claim that I am an authority on the doctrine of Christianity. Therefore, I am not qualified to write a religious book. *The Politics of the Crucifixion* is not a religious book in any way.

I do know something about the dynamics of politics, however, and it was the political motivations of both supporters and opponents of Jesus that led me to author *The Politics of the Crucifixion*.

Let me note one thing before going on. Here in the United States, we equate politics with popular elections. However, politics is just as prevalent in those nations that do not practice free elections as it is in those that do. In fact, it is often more prevalent. In those lands without popular elections, politicians are just as likely react to public pressures as are elected politicians elsewhere. Therefore, even though voters did not elect Roman Governors or Judean Kings, those rulers were not immune to politics. On the contrary, Roman and Judean rulers allowed ordinary citizens to sway them at every turn.

The political pressures bearing down on Herod and Pilate made the execution of Jesus impossible to avoid. Herod feared that making Jesus a martyr and Pilate loathed executing an innocent man. Yet, the enemies of Jesus, and the mob they gathered around them, refused to allow these powerful men to leave Jesus alive.

Politics infected those that followed Jesus as well. The *Gospels* illustrate the political motivations of the Apostles. The motivations the Apostles (often as petty and ugly as those of the opponents of Jesus) were in some ways just as much a cause of the crucifixion as were the motivations of the Judeans and the Romans.

While I understand that writing about Jesus and the crucifixion in political terms may offend some Christians, I do not believe that the truth should ever offend anyone. In addition, I sincerely hope that this book will aid in increasing the general understanding of the message Jesus brought – and continues to bring – to a troubled world.

CL Gammon, July 26, 2015

# Introduction

Jesus came into the material world as a pre-ordained king. Others, not he, proclaimed him to be of royal stock. However, when he felt the time was right, he accepted the kingly mantle and proclaimed the coming kingdom of which he would head.

Jesus knew that proclaiming himself the true king was a dangerous thing. This did not bother him; he had lived his entire life under the threat of death. From his birth, his enemies had sought to murder him. He accepted the possibly that he might be executed at any moment, and despite unrelenting threats to his well-being, he continued to spread his message of the coming kingdom.

*The Politics of the Crucifixion* deals with the efforts of the enemies of Jesus to prevent him from attaining the Judean throne, but it does more than that. This book also looks at the political motivations of the many groups that opposed Jesus. In addition, it looks at the political motivations at play among those supporting Jesus, especially the twelve major disciples of Jesus – referred to here as the Apostles.

The author relies on the *Gospels*, to follow the chain of events from the birth of Jesus until his crucifixion. Of course, the author consulted non-biblical sources for pertinent information as well.

The author employed the *King James Version of the Bible* in the writing of this book.

The reason for this is that the *King James Version* is the most beautiful literary translation of the Bible in English and, frankly, the author has an affinity for it.

The author lists the birth of Jesus as 4 BC. Some scholars disagree with this date. However, no other date fits the events mentioned in the *Gospels*. It fits the census before the Census of Quirinius mentioned by historians and in the book of *Luke*. It fits the known date of Herod the Great's death. It fits all other biblical and historical references as well.

Some scholars believe that Jesus could have been born before 4 BC, possibly as early as 6 BC. However, these scholars base this contention on Herod's order to murder of all Bethlehem's children two years old, or older. Of course, Herod's order did not indicate that the target of his order was two-years old, it merely means that he did not know exactly how old Jesus was and that he was not taking any chances.

The author hopes that this book gives readers a better insight into the events that caused Judean leaders to reject Jesus and those political factors that led him to his execution by Roman authorities.

# 1. The Paranoid King Herod

Herod the Great sat upon the throne of Judea in 4 BC, but nervously so. He had come to be rule Judea in an illegal way and, thus, he was never secure in his reign.

The murder of Julius Caesar in 44 BC threw the Roman world into chaos. Herod used this chaos to aid him in his climb to power in 37 BC. First, King Herod sided with Mark Antony and the Egyptian Queen Cleopatra, but when Augustus defeated Antony and Cleopatra, and assumed the title of Emperor, Herod gladly became one of the Caesar's strongest supporters in the Middle East. In exchange for his support, Augustus allowed Herod to remain in his position as King of Judea. However, Caesar did not completely trust Herod and he also appointed a Roman Governor to oversee the area.

While Herod the Great was, in essence, a glorified figurehead King, the Romans allowed him to make decisions that did not directly conflict with Imperial objectives in the area. Thus, Herod had great power over his subjects and he exercised this power with great vigor. However, Herod's acts were inconsistent and they varied from the most ambitious building projects to the cruelest murders.

As described earlier, even though Herod had the greatest military power on earth propping him up, he never felt secure upon the Judean throne. There were several reasons for this. Firstly, he had obtained the crown illegally. His climb to power came without the support of the people he subsequently ruled. Secondly, Herod was not truly Jewish, although he attempted to act as if he were. Herod was actually Arab (*Kasher, Aryeh, King Herod: A Persecuted Persecutor*). Herod's position as an outsider and a usurper made him unpopular with most of his subjects.

Herod also had to deal with the fact that throughout his reign rumors persisted that the legitimate King of Judea of whom they awaited was about to appear (*Isaiah 9:6*).

The rumors worried the already paranoid Herod to no end. However, he could do nothing about them except to formulate plans to murder the true king if, and when, he appeared.

## 2. The Rival to Herod Arrives

One day in the spring of 4 BC, a messenger burst into Herod's residence with news that important foreign visitors from the East – perhaps kings – were in Jerusalem inquiring as to the residence of the new King of Judea that had been, or soon would be, born (*Matthew 2:1-2*). The news greatly troubled Herod and those that depended on him for their wealth and power (*Matthew 2:3*).

It was, and is, unusual for important foreign visitors to enter other nations without requesting an audience with the leaders of those nations. That the visitors from the East did not request an audience with Herod naturally caused him to suspect them.

Before we go on, it is important to establish that it was natural for the kings came to come to Jerusalem seeking the new King of Judea. Jerusalem was the capital of Judea. Therefore, it made sense that the young king would be living there. Yet, the visiting kings had to know that the new king was not of the house of Herod. If they had believed that, they would have inquired at Herod's palace immediately. Thus, Herod's paranoia was somewhat justified, because this time the proclamation of the new King of Judea was more than an idle rumor.

Herod did not overreact and have the Easterners arrested and killed. Such a rash act could have caused problems with his Roman masters. They would not have tolerated the murder of foreign dignitaries without prior approval from the Imperial Governor. Instead, Herod decided to befriend the foreigners and to use them to locate the young king for him.

Before Herod met with the foreigners, he brought in his experts on Judean law and inquired as to where the true king was to be born. The experts responded that according to tradition, the place would be home town of David, tiny, insignificant Bethlehem of Judea. (*Micah 5:2*) Having satisfied himself that he knew the city where the true king likely resided, Herod was ready to make his next move (*Matthew 2:4-5*).

Herod requested a private conference with the foreign kings that were searching for the new king. Of course, the foreigners came before him as quickly as they could. Herod was polite to the kings and treated them with the respect that visitors of such importance deserved. He informed his guests that his experts predicted that the new king was to be born in Bethlehem of Judea and he encouraged them to go there and pay their respects to the child. In addition, he requested that afterwards the kings return to Jerusalem and give him exact location of the young king so that he could pay his respects as well (*Matthew 2:7-8*).

The foreigners were pleased that Herod intended to accept the new king. Of course, they had no idea that Herod was using them to locate the king for him so he could murder his rival. They promised Herod that they would return with the information he wanted and then, they happily left the palace and began the six mile journey due south from Jerusalem to Bethlehem. (*Matthew 2:9*)

We can speculate that Herod did not send agents with the foreigners because he did not desire to alert the visiting kings to his true plan. However, word of his true intentions did leak out anyway.

## 3. Jesus Escapes Herod

The foreigners, the Bible does not list a number as to how many there were, continued to Bethlehem and located the baby Jesus and his mother Mary. The easterners never had any doubt that they had found the rightful King of Judea. They were correct. Jesus was a direct descendant of David and the throne of Judea was legally his by his birthright (*Matthew 1:17*).

Jesus came to be born in Bethlehem because Emperor Augustus had ordered a general census so that Roman could levy a new tax its citizens. Historians refer to this event as the census before the Census of Quirinius. Some scholars say that hold that this census occurred in the year 6 BC. However, the best sources confirm that it actually began in the year 4 BC (*Encyclopaedia Biblica: A Critical Dictionary of the Literary, Political and Religion History, the Archeology, Geography and Natural History of the Bible*).

The head of each household was required to return to his family's traditional hometown. Since Joseph was a direct descendant of David, he took Mary, his very pregnant wife, to David's hometown of Bethlehem. Jesus was thus born there. Of course, the place of his birth was another proof that Jesus was the rightful King of Judea (*Luke 2:1-12*).

After the foreign visitors located Jesus, they paid homage to him as if he already sat upon the Judean throne. They presented the enfant monarch with kingly treasures of expensive spices, oils and even gold (*Matthew 2:11*).

Of course, the previous direct descendants of David had been entitled to rule as well, but they had lived politically obscure lives for several generations and drew no notice from the kings of Judea or from Judean religious leaders. Even Herod the Great knew nothing of them. However, that changed with the birth of Jesus.

After paying homage to Jesus, the kings retired for the evening and they intended to return to Jerusalem the next morning. However, before the kings departed from Bethlehem, they learned it was Herod's true intention to murder the enfant king. Of course, they had no desire to aid Herod in his murderous plan, so they chose to thwart him by avoiding Jerusalem and another conference with the monarch. They quietly and quickly left Herod's domain without his knowledge (*Matthew 2:12*).

Joseph too learned of Herod's intention to find and murder Jesus. Joseph collected his family's possessions hurriedly and transported Mary and Jesus to Egypt as quickly as he could (*Matthew 2:13-14*).

Egypt was a logical place for Joseph to relocate his family. It was in close proximity to Judea and in many ways, the two locales were alike. Joseph could practice his trade as a builder there. Egypt was part of the Roman Empire and that would ease the turmoil a move would cause. Yet, Herod had neither power nor influence in Egypt. Remaining in Egypt would guarantee that Joseph and his family would remain safe.

However, Joseph did not intend to make Egypt his family's permanent home. Herod had grown old and Joseph was certain that the evil king, who was well past sixty years of age, would soon be dead, thus relieving the threat to Jesus. Joseph planned to return to Judea as soon as Herod died (*Matthew 2:15*).

# 4. Massacre of the Innocents

Herod the Great, called "the evil genius of the Judean nation" was viciously murderous even for ancient times (*Heinrich Graetz, History of the Jews*). He had no problem with killing all those he considered his enemies. He even ordered the murder of several of his sons because he feared that they might usurp his reign. Another example of his insane disregard for others was his order to have the leading men of Judea killed just to fulfill his vanity (*Josephus Flavius, Jewish Antiquities*).

Word of the departure of the kings did not reach Herod for some time. When Herod learned that the foreigners had exited Judea without his knowledge, he flew into the greatest paranoid rage of his life. He knew he could not get at the foreigners, but he could still eliminate his rival. Herod ordered his soldiers to descend upon Bethlehem and kill the young king. Since Herod had no way of positively identifying his rival, he demanded the murder of every child in Bethlehem of two years old and younger (*Matthew 2:16-18*).

Herod's soldiers complied with his orders and rushed to Bethlehem with great haste, but Herod's delay in sending them meant that they arrived too late to get at Jesus. Joseph had already saved his family by packing up his belongings and secreting Mary and Jesus off toward Egypt. Herod's soldiers, of course, did not know that the child they sought had already departed. They went about their grim task and slaughtered the first born of the city (*Matthew 2: 15-18*).

Some question whether Herod actually slaughtered the children of Bethlehem They wonder why, if the murders occurred, did most 1st Century historians ignore the event.

To the doubters, the author offers this: The account of Herod ordering the murder of the sons of Bethlehem to protect his power is right in character for him. Thus, no one can doubt that he would do such a thing without any qualms. During that time, the population of Bethlehem was likely not over 300, and perhaps even fewer than that. Therefore, the total number of children killed in the tiny town would have been less than ten. Certainly, the number of children murdered at Bethlehem was not great enough to rank anywhere near the top of the list of Herod's many murder sprees. Thus, this minor slaughter failed to make it into most historical records (*R. T. France, The New International Commentary on the New Testament – The Gospel of Matthew*).

## 5. Jesus Returns to Judea

Joseph was correct in his assessment that the murderer king Herod the Great would soon be dead. Herod the Great died within a year of the birth of Jesus and when Joseph learned the would-be tormenter of the true king was dead; he again took up all that he owned and prepared to return to Judea (*Matthew 2:19-21*).

This trip had to make Joseph and Mary happy. First, Herod could not persecute Jesus from the grave and second, the family was returning to the familiar environs of home. Yes, this move had to be a happy event.

However, not everything was as Joseph hoped it would be. Upon reentering Judea, Joseph did not know if the new ruler would attempt to kill Jesus as Herod the Great had, but Joseph could not take the risk. Instead of settling near Jerusalem, Joseph took his family through Galilee and settled it back in Nazareth. (*Matthew 2:22-23*).

Nazareth is only about sixty miles north of Jerusalem, but Joseph believed that Jesus would be safe as long as the family led a quiet life and avoided any political controversy. This proved to be true. Except for the fact that Jesus displayed an extraordinary intelligence and that Mary and Joseph feared constantly for his safety, he had an uneventful childhood (*Luke 2:47-48*).

Jesus learned the building trade from Joseph (*Mark 6:3*) and was evidently very successful at it. Thus, a happy and prosperous

Jesus lived well into adulthood before he drew the attention of the latest false King of Judea (*Matthew 13:55*).

# 6. John Preaches the Kingdom

The idea that a new King of Judea would soon appear persisted for decades after the birth of Jesus. The rumors of the new king coming were everywhere. However, one man stood out in his proclaiming of the coming king.

John the Baptist was a cousin of Jesus. In addition, he had been born a mere six months before Jesus. John the Baptist became the leading proponent of the coming kingdom (*Matthew 3:1-3*).

John loudly proclaimed the coming king before large crowds and he became one of the most famous men in Judea, and especially, in the region around the Jordan River where he baptized thousands of converts (*Matthew 3:5-6*).

Evidently, some of John's followers came to believe that he might be the true King of Judea. Confronted with this, John had to end the speculation. He made a point of telling his followers that he was not the king that the people expected to appear. John did not attempt to identify the coming king by name or even say that he knew the identity of the king. However, he did promise that the king would appear soon and that this king would be a truly great man (*Matthew 3:11-12*).

John was a large and imposing man. In addition, he was a natural leader in that he held strong views and he expressed them boldly. However, he was not the wild-eyed, uneducated rabble-rouser some portray him to be. On the contrary, John the Baptist was a product of a priestly family and he was well versed in Judean religious rules and regulations. His background and undeniable knowledge of Judean law gave John's words weight among those who heard him (*Luke 1:5-25*). In addition, his uncompromising stances on all matters energized his disciples. Of course, John was a danger to those representing the status quo.

# 7. John Faces Opposition

John's preaching of the coming kingdom caused him to run into difficulties with the two most important of the many political-religious factions in Judea, the Pharisees and Sadducees. The dispute between John and his adversaries soon became bitter and personal. John, who never minced words, did not conceal his contempt for his opponents. He went so far as to compare the Pharisees and Sadducees to venomous snakes (*Matthew 3:7*).

While both the Pharisees and Sadducees opposed John's version of what the coming kingdom, that does not mean that they agreed with each other on either political or religious matters. On the contrary, the two sects were bitter opponents.

The Pharisees were elitists who attempted to separate themselves from ordinary Judeans. Over time, the Pharisees came to adopt a superior attitude towards their fellows. This attitude caused a gulf to develop between the Pharisees and the majority of Judeans. Many Judeans shared the view of later Roman historian Flavius Josephus. He condemned the Pharisees as heretics (*Josephus Flavius, Jewish Antiquities*).

Beyond the separation issues, the Pharisees came to believe that only they practiced pure Judaism and that all others practiced a corrupted version of the faith.

On the political side, the Pharisees went so far as to claim that they deserved to "sit in the seat of Moses." In other words, they believed that they should control the political and religious fate of Judea. The Pharisees also contended that only they could speak with authority concerning matters requiring scriptural interpretation.

Of course, the arrogant and conceited views of the Pharisees were utterly incompatible to the belief that a single king would arise and save Judea. While the Pharisees were not generally great supporters of Herod, and they almost universally opposed Roman domination of Judea, they evidently saw John and his kingdom doctrine as more dangerous to them than were their other opponents. Thus, many Pharisees were willing to use Herod and the Romans to rid them of the hated Baptist.

The Sadducees were the chief political and religious opponents of the Pharisees in Judea. The Sadducees rejected the contention of the Pharisees that the interpretation of the law and following tradition were paramount. Instead, they believed in following the strict letter of the law. Because of this, the Sadducees became the party of the Jewish Priests.

The Sadducees were willing to work with Herod and the Romans in exchange for a powerful role in Judea. Of course, John's sermons proclaiming the coming of a new king stood to dislodge the Sadducees from their powerful perch. Most Judeans respected the Sadducees, in religious matters, but the Sadducees' fawning at the feet of the Romans caused many Judeans to consider them as traitors. Flavius Josephus identified the

Sadducees as heretics as well (*Josephus Flavius, Jewish Antiquities*).

For years, the Pharisees and Sadducees contested with each other for the religious and political domination of Judea. That contest included a constant battle over the most important Judean political-religious court, the "Sanhedrin" (*The New Compact Bible Dictionary, edited by T. Alton Bryant*).

Even though the Pharisees and Sadducees were bitter political enemies, both parties despised and feared John's doctrine of the coming kingdom and they formed an uneasy and temporary alliance to try to stifle his message.

Despite, or maybe because of, the alignment of his powerful enemies against him, the fame of John the Baptist grew and spread across Judea at an even faster rate than before.

Then one day, Jesus approached and requested that John baptize him. John realized that Jesus was the true King of Judea he had awaited. John balked at baptizing Jesus at first because he felt unworthy to do it. However, Jesus prevailed and after John baptized him, Jesus was ready to begin preaching the coming of kingdom himself (*Matthew 3:13-17*).

# 8. John is Arrested

Herod Antipas (21 BC-39 AD), called the Tetrarch because he ruled only a portion of his father's former kingdom, came to the throne in 4 BC after his father expired. (*Josephus Flavius, Jewish Antiquities*) The younger Herod, like his father, never felt secure in his rule. Thus, it is no surprise that John the Baptist would soon earn the ire of the Judean ruler.

The younger Herod ordered the arrest of John the Baptist because John had denounced Herod's marriage to Herodias. Herodias (about 15 BC-After 39 AD) was the daughter of Aristobulus. Aristobulus was a son of Herod the Great. This made the young Herod Antipas Herodias's uncle.

Herodias married another of her uncles, named Philip. Herod Antipas, the Tetrarch, visited Philip and Herodias and became infatuated with his half brother's wife. Herod convinced Herodias to return to Judea with him and become his queen. He then divorced his legal wife and married his niece Herodias.

John correctly pointed out that the royal marriage was illegal under Judean law and he demanded that Herod return Herodias to her rightful husband, Philip. The Baptist's remarks infuriated Herod and the king desired to take hold of John and to execute him. However, Herod feared that putting one as popular as the Baptist to death would cause unrest, and possibly a revolution, in Judea. Therefore, the king ordered John arrested and kept in prison without trial until he could decide what to do with the troublesome precursor (*Matthew 14:3-5*).

## 9. John is Executed

As stated earlier, Herod feared that killing John the Baptist would cause unrest, or even a revolt. This was a reasonable assumption for Herod to make. Of course, a rebellion could topple him from his throne. Even if the Judean people did not overthrow him with a revolution, his Roman masters would likely not stand for a king that caused revolt among his people. There were already Judeans openly revolting against the Romans and the Empire did not need more problems.

The Zealots were the most important faction of the Judean revolutionaries. (*Josephus Flavius, Jewish Antiquities*) While the Zealots could not reasonably hope to break Roman power in Judea, they were a distinct nuisance. The Zealots were responsible for the murder of Roman soldiers and other political crimes. If the followers of John the Baptist united with the Zealots, the threat to the Empire would increase exponentially. Herod could not risk the disfavor of Rome, so he avoided deciding John's fate for as long as he could.

Yet, Herod could not make his wife understand his dilemma. Herodias could never feel safe as long as John lived. She knew that John would continue his campaign against her marriage to Herod, even from his prison cell. Herodias pressured Herod to execute John and remove the obstacle the Baptist represented to her reign with her husband in Judea.

Herod was a weak monarch indeed. Despite much reasoning, refusing and protesting, his resistance eventually gave way. Herod went against his better judgment, relented to Herodias and ordered John beheaded. As proof of the brutal act, Herod had John's head delivered to the royal household on a platter (*Matthew 14:6-11*).

John's disciples collected his body – Herod refused to surrender John's head – and they buried it. Then, they found Jesus and informed him of John's execution (*Matthew 14:12*).

# 10. Jesus Locates his Apostles

When Jesus was ready, he began the process of preaching his coming kingdom. However, he knew that he could not accomplish his mission without help, so he recruited lieutenants to aid him in his mission. He charged his twelve most senior aids, called Apostles here, with spreading his kingdom message throughout Judea and the surrounding area before his crucifixion.

In this chapter, the author briefly profiles each of the twelve Apostles and their activities before the execution of Jesus. One note: Though the *Gospels* often list all the Apostles together, Jesus did not locate all his Apostles in one place, or at the same time. In addition, Jesus added some of his Apostles only after he began preaching the kingdom doctrine.

## Simon Peter

Simon Peter was born at the fishing village of Bethsaida, which was about 80 miles from Jerusalem (*John 1:42, 44*). In his youth, he moved to the larger, but nearby, town of Capharnaum with his family (*Matthew 8:14*).

Simon Peter had a wife and children and he was a successful in the fishing business (*Luke 5:3*), but he was drawn to the kingdom sermons preached by John the Baptist. Soon, Simon Peter became one of the Baptist's leading disciples. However, Simon Peter left John and joined Jesus, upon his first meeting with the rightful king. After that, Simon Peter remained close to Jesus up until the Judean religious leaders took the true king of Judea into custody (*John 2:4*).

Jesus granted Simon Peter the first place among the Apostles and it is apparent that Simon Peter acted as Christ's bodyguard (*Matthew 16:18*). The author provides more information on the promotion of Simon Peter in Chapter 16.

## Andrew

Andrew was Simon Peter's brother and they grew up together (*John 1:44, Matthew 10:2*). Like Simon Peter, Andrew was in the fishing business and was a disciple of John the Baptist (*Matthew 4:18, John 1:35-40*).

Andrew met Jesus and immediately recognized him as the king that the Judeans had awaited for so long (*John 1:41*). He introduced Jesus and Peter and then, he and his brother became Apostles of Jesus.

The *Gospels* mention Andrew only a few times, however, it is safe for us to assume that Jesus entrusted Andrew with several important assignments because when is always among the first four Apostles named (*Matthew 10:2-4*).

## James the Greater

James the Greater was one of two Apostles named James. This James was called "the Greater' most likely because he was larger and taller than the other Apostle named James. James the Greater was the son of Zebedee (*Matthew 27:56*). He was the older brother of Apostle John. James the Greater was of priestly origins in that his grandfather on his mother's side served as a Jewish Priest. James the Greater was in the fishing business like his father (*John 1:44*).

Like John the Baptist, James the Greater was a cousin of Jesus (*John 19:25, Matthew 27:56, Mark 15:40*).

James the Greater was loud, outgoing and had a nasty temper. For this reason, those that knew him as one of the "sons of thunder" (*Mark 3:17*).

James the Greater was undecided at first as to leave his profession and join Jesus. However, his brother John persuaded him to become an Apostle.

As ambivalent as he was at first, James the Greater had ambition and he attempted to acquire a guarantee from Jesus of a preferred place in the kingdom (*Mark 10:37*). Jesus declined to provide the guarantee James the Greater of the highest place in the kingdom. However, Jesus did promise James the Greater a role in his government (*Mark 10:38-39*).

## John

Apostle John was the younger brother of James the Greater. He shared many things in common with his brother. He was loud in his proclamations concerning the coming kingdom and was one of the sons of thunder. He was ambitions and attempted – and failed – to gain preferred status in the kingdom (*Mark 10:37-38*). He fished for a living with his brother and his father Zebedee before he joined the kingdom movement (*John 1:44*).

However, John was more prominent among the Apostles than was James the Greater (*Luke 22:8*). In fact, biblical evidence indicates that John was the second most important Apostle (*John 13:23, 25*).

Ironically, when Jesus approached James the Greater and John, their father was with them. Either Jesus did not ask Zebedee to join the Apostles, or Zebedee refused. There is no evidence as to how Zebedee felt about his sons leaving the family business, but he did not stop them from going with Jesus (*Matthew 4:21-22*).

## Philip

Like Simon Peter and Andrew, the Apostle Philip resided at Bethsaida. Bethsaida was a fishing village on the other side of the sea from Galilee (*Luke 8:26*). In addition, like Simon Peter and Andrew, Philip observed the doctrine of John the Baptist Before meeting Jesus.

The *Gospel of John* indicates that Philip was a strong believer, but that he lacked self-confidence (*John 6:5-7; 12:21-23; and 14:8-9*). While there are several mentions of Philip in the *Gospels*, his shyness seems to have preventing him from becoming a leader among his fellow Apostles.

## Bartholomew

We know little of substance about the activities of Bartholomew before Jesus suffered crucifixion. Some scholars even claim that others named in the *Gospels* were, in fact, Bartholomew. It seems that Jesus never entrusted Bartholomew with any important tasks to perform alone. What we do know without doubt was that he was Judean. We can also surmise that he hailed from Galilee, as did a great many of the other Apostles.

## Thomas Didymus

We know Thomas Didymus as the Apostle who doubted that Jesus had risen from the dead (*John 20:25*). This and other biblical references to Thomas Didymus indicate that he was skeptical by nature and that he was somewhat argumentative (*John 14:15*). Yet, he was also one of the most faithful of the Apostles. He stated his willingness to give his life for the cause of the kingdom long before any of the other Apostles did (*John 11:16*).

## Matthew the Tax Collector

Matthew (also called Levi) was a tax collector by trade (*Matthew 9:9*). He was the son of Alpheus (*Mark 2:14*) and he lived and worked at Capharnaum, but he may have been Syrian by birth. It is not strange that a Syrian collected Judean taxes for two reasons: (1) after the Romans conquered the area, "foreigners" flooded into it from across the Middle East and (2) Judeans hated tax collectors so much that "locals" avoided taking the job.

## James the Lesser

Apostle James the Lesser (called so because of his small stature in comparison to the other Apostle named James) was the son of a man named Alpheus. Apostle Matthew's father was also called Alpheus, however, James the Lesser and Matthew were not brothers; their fathers simply carried the same name. James the

Lesser was the brother of the Apostle Jude, however (*Matthew 10:3*).

James the Lesser was of a pious Judean family and he was well versed in Judean religious law.

### Jude (Thaddaeus Lebbaeus, Judas)

Apostle Jude (Also called Thaddaeus Lebbaeus and Judas) was the brother of James the Lesser. Like his brother James the Lesser, Jude authored a book of the current Bible (*Matthew 10:3*).

Jude was no doubt a lesser light than most of the other Apostles. He was certainly less famous than his brother James the Lesser. This is apparent from the fact that Jude generally identified himself as the brother of James.

### Simon the Canaanite

Simon the Canaanite was a lesser Apostle. The *Gospels* seldom mention Simon the Canaanite (*Matthew 10:4*). Yet, according to what the other Apostles called him, he was zealous in his support of Judean law.

Some hold that because the *Gospels* refer to Simon the Canaanite as "the Zealot", that he was a member of the revolutionary religious-political party called the Zealots (*Luke 6:15*). Others hold that this is entirely untrue. As stated earlier, the Zealots were a revolutionary party that endeavored to drive the Romans out of Judea by force. They engaged in acts of terror and murder and considered themselves engaged in a war with the Romans. Those that deny that Simon was a member of the Zealots state that Jesus would never have allowed such a person to be an Apostle. However, Jesus never rejected anyone because of his past and would have certainly embraced a reformed Zealot as quickly as he would have embraced like any other sinner.

### Judas Iscariot

As one would expect, the *Gospels* always speak of Judas Iscariot in terms of his betrayal of Jesus and then his suicide (*Matthew 10:4; Matthew 27:5*). However, we do have some other information about Judas Iscariot as well.

Judas Iscariot was born in the south of Judea at a town called Kerioth. Kerioth is only about 32 miles south of Jerusalem; however, in the first century, it was off the beaten path. The fact that Judas Iscariot was the only one of the first 12 Apostles not to be a Galilean may have had an effect on his later actions – more about that later.

The Gospels always list Judas Iscariot last among the Apostles. However, one should not assume that he was always at the bottom of the chain of power among the Apostles. In fact, as the holder of the moneybox, he held a powerful and responsible role in the Apostle hierarchy. The *Gospels* list Judas Iscariot last in the order of Apostles because he betrayed Jesus, not because he was a minor Apostle.

It is probable that Judas Iscariot was an accountant by trade. This can explain why Jesus entrusted him with the monies earmarked for use in the ministry. The *Gospels* do not confirm this directly, but this explains why Jesus would give him such an important task. The author presents more about Judas Iscariot in Chapters 21 and 22.

# 11. Jesus Preaches His Kingdom

After John baptized him and he began putting together his group of Apostles, Jesus traveled throughout the area in and around Judea and preached that the founding of the legal kingdom was coming in the near future (*Mark 1:14-15*).

Jesus took every opportunity to preach in synagogues and other places where pious Judean citizens congregated. Ordinary Judeans, that is, those not belonging to the major political-religious sects, received his message with enthusiasm. In addition, most of John the Baptist's Disciples joined the movement headed by Jesus. In a short time, Jesus gained fame throughout Judea, Syria, the Greek cities comprising the Decapolis and beyond the Jordan River. Jesus even became famous in Jerusalem, though he had not yet preached his kingdom message there (*Matthew 4:13, 17, 23-24*).

Massive crowds congregated around Jesus wherever he went. This made it necessary for him to find unique methods to preach to his followers. On one such occasion, he climbed upon a large hill to speak to the throng collected in his midst. Appropriately, today we refer to this speech as the "Sermon on the Mount" (*Matthew 5:1*).

During the Sermon on the Mount, Jesus gave his audience an idea of what his kingdom would be like. In addition, he told them who would populate it. He promised a place for the poor in spirit (and the poor financially as well).

He promised comfort for those in pain. He promised a place for the oppressed. He offered to fill the hungry "in spirit". Jesus also promised a special place in his kingdom for the merciful, the pure in heart, the peacemakers and the persecuted (*Matthew 5:2-12*).

Having described the coming kingdom, Jesus sought to explain that he was no great revolutionary. He told his audience that he did not intend to destroy the traditional order, but to reestablish it. Jesus commanded his followers to obey the ancient law of Judea without deviation in any way. In fact, he ordered his followers to observe the law to a greater degree than did the Pharisees and the Sadducees (*Matthew 5:17-20*).

Next, Jesus took the opportunity of teaching the proper method of prayer. He did this for two reasons. First, he intended to appease the followers of John the Baptist that had joined his movement. These disciples of John the Baptist desired Jesus to teach team as John had taught them (*Luke 11:1*).

More importantly, Jesus reinforced the concept that the coming kingdom not only had the full approval of God, it would be a model of God's heavenly kingdom. Jesus said that at the establishment of the kingdom earthly acts would mirror heavenly acts. Jesus also indicated that the kingdom would acquire its strength from the power and glory of God (*Matthew 6:10, 13*).

Jesus did not claim openly to be the coming king during the Sermon on the Mount. However, he spoke with such authority that many in the crowd understood that they were looking at the true King of Judea (*Matthew 7:28-29*).

## 12. Jesus Amplifies His Message

Jesus amplified his kingdom message to both his Apostles and other followers several times. Once Jesus told a story about a servant who owed a king a great sum of money. The king demanded his money and the servant did not have it. The servant begged the king not to imprison him, but to allow him time to repay the debt. The king felt compassion for the servant and forgave the debt completely (*Matthew 18:23-27*).

Later, the servant whom the king had just forgiven went to a man who owed him a small amount and demanded *his* money. The poor man who owed the small debt could not repay it. He begged that he be given time to make good on the loan. However, the king's servant refused and had the authorities throw the poor man into prison (*Matthew 18:28-30*).

Some other servants went to the king and told him what had happened. Of course, the king was outraged. The king then ordered the reinstatement of the servant's debts and ordered the servant imprisoned until he repaid all he owed (*Matthew 18:31-35*).

Thus, according to Jesus, the kingdom would be a place of forgiveness for those willing to forgive. However, those that had no forgiveness in them would receive their just punishment

Jesus told his Apostles that it was nearly, but not completely impossible for the rich to reside in his kingdom (*Matthew 19:23-26*).

The above illustrates that Jesus believed that the accumulation of great wealth required such single-mindedness that everything else would be set aside. Of course, if the man building riches had no dedication to the kingdom, he could not enter. Yet, according to Jesus, if the rich man would find a way to put the kingdom first, he could enter.

On another occasion, Jesus explained that his kingdom would be one of equality. He told a long story about a man who hired several employees at different times during a day, but paid them all the same wage. Thus, Jesus illustrated that he would view all the citizens of his kingdom as equals regardless of their status. Nor did he care when they joined the movement or entered the kingdom. He also applied this idea of equity to his Apostles. With the exception of Simon Peter, Jesus refused to rank them in order of importance officially (*Matthew 20 1-14*). (See Chapter 17)

Jesus told another long story explaining what his kingdom would be like. The message of that story is simple. The Judean leaders and upper classes would refuse to accept the kingdom and because of that, they would lose the power over the ordinary citizens that they currently enjoyed. Then, Jesus would offer the Gentiles and lower classes the opportunity to enter the kingdom, if they met certain specific conditions (*Matthew 22:1-14*).

Jesus told another story cautioning his followers to prepare for the coming of the kingdom, because he might assume the throne it at any time. Jesus continued that only those who had prepared for the coming kingdom could enter. He made a point of telling his followers to be wise and to avoid silly and foolish things (*Matthew 25:1-13*).

After the death of Herod the Great, the Romans approved the dividing of his kingdom between his sons. Jesus used the memory of this event to bring Judeans to his cause. He told them that he did not come to divide Judea, but to unify it. He continued that the fact that he was a unifier proved that he was the rightful king (*Matthew 12:25, 28, 42*).

## 13. Jesus and His Government

Jesus could not establish his kingdom alone. Thus, he formed a multi-layered government to aid him. While the *Gospels* mention the 12 Apostles most often, he also appointed lesser members of his government. In a short time, these lesser officials totaled at least 70 and Jesus gave them special tasks as well (*Luke 10:1-12*). Shortly after the Romans executed Jesus, the number of lesser Disciples had grown to at least 120 (*Acts 1:15*).

While sometimes, Jesus specifically issued orders to the lesser Disciples, they were subordinate to the 12 Apostles and received orders from them as well.

Jesus usually spoke to his audiences in the form of simple stories. When his Apostles questioned as to why he did this, he replied that the masses were not yet prepared to receive complete information concerning the kingdom, but that his Apostles were (*Matthew 13:10-12, 19*).

Jesus continued that even though he spoke to them in plain language, not all of his Apostles would understand his message about the kingdom. Jesus finished that if Apostles failed to understand the true nature of the kingdom, they would become tools for the opposition (*Matthew 13:10-12, 19*).

Jesus spoke about the kingdom by telling his followers a story about a wheat field that had weeds in it. In the story, the landowner refused to try to rid the weeds because to do so would also damage the wheat as well. In this parable, Jesus made the point that his reign would not be one of war, murder and violence as was Herod's reign. On the contrary, Jesus portrayed his kingdom as one of tolerance and protection of the innocent (*Matthew 13:24-30*).

Jesus also described his kingdom as being tiny – like a mustard seed -- but he predicted it that it would blossom, grow and flourish into the greatest nation ever known (*Matthew 13:31-32*).

Of course, Jesus was comparing the size of little Judea to the grandeur of the Rome. It must have startled his listeners that he envisioned the rise of a kingdom larger than the Roman Empire. It must have energized them as well.

Jesus told his followers that they should not wonder as to the how he would found the kingdom, but that they should busy themselves with being prepared to serve in it when he established it. If they had prepared for it, they would reap its benefits when the time was right (*Mark 4:26-30*).

Jesus continued that the kingdom was coming to power very soon indeed. Thus, it was important for them to be ready for it (*Mark 9:1*).

Jesus told his Apostles that they should consider anyone who did not directly oppose them as an ally. He ordered them to promise the rewards of his kingdom to anyone who gave them even the most nominal aid (*Mark 9:40-*

41). On the other hand, Jesus promised to punish any and all that directly opposed the establishment of his kingdom or did violence to any of his followers (*Mark 9:42*).

Jesus also forbade his followers from placing obstacles in front of those who desired to join his movement. He made it clear that he was not interested in just having followers who understood the mechanisms of the kingdom, but also those came into it through faith alone (*Mark 10:14-15*).

In several stories, Jesus compared his kingdom to something more valuable than the greatest treasures on earth. He compared it to gold or pearls for which one would sell all he owned to purchase and possess (*Matthew 13:44-46*).

Jesus then called together his Apostles and instructed them to oppose the political and religious doctrines of the Pharisees and the Sadducees (*Matthew 16:6, 12*). He did this because the tradition Judean leaders stood in variance to the true law.

Jesus demanded that his Apostles be fully committed to him. He told them that they must be willing to die for him and his kingdom. In exchange for their fidelity, he would reward them in the kingdom, when he established himself upon the throne (*Matthew 16:25-28*).

## 14. Jesus Defines his Kingdom

After Jesus had appointed his government officials, it was important for him to identify himself as the true king of the Judeans and that his Apostles would be leaders in his kingdom. That was his next order of business. The act of defining his government was extremely important.

John the Baptist may have been convinced that Jesus was the true king, but not all of John's followers were. They often questioned the actions and motives of Jesus. On one occasion, some of John's followers asked Jesus why his followers did not fast when those of John did. Jesus answered in a way that illustrated that he was the king and that his Apostles and other Disciples were members of his government. Jesus replied that there was no need for his Apostles or other Disciples to fast as long as he was with them. However, he continued that when he was no longer there, then they would fast (*Matthew 9:14-17*). However, not even his Apostles understood that he was telling them that he would soon to depart from them.

Jesus continued the theme that his twelve Apostles were to be leaders of his kingly government. He told them to avoid Gentiles and Samaritans, for the time being, and to concentrate on winning over the Judeans to his kingdom doctrine first (*Matthew 10:5-7*).

Jesus desired that his Apostles know that their lot would be a difficult one. He told them that other "Governors and Kings" would persecute them brutally because of their association with him (*Matthew 10:18*). Jesus continued that they would be the most hated persons on earth due to their promotion of the kingdom doctrine (*Matthew 10:22*). By elevating his Apostles to the level of "Governors and Kings", Jesus let them know their importance in the kingdom. However, he tempered that by again telling them the degree of opposition they would face.

Jesus stated that his Apostles should not overly engage those who hated the kingdom doctrine. He said that when his enemies persecuted them in one city that they should abandon it, go to another city, and preach there (*Matthew 10:23*). His point was that the mission of the Apostles was to gain converts, not to overcome enemies.

Jesus left no doubt that he was in charge. He established himself as the ruler of Judea in all matters. Jesus told his Apostles that he was the sole authority in both religious and political matters (*Matthew 12:8*).

Jesus informed his Apostles that simply being loyal followers was not good enough. He ordered them to endeavor to use every opportunity to recruit new converts to reside in the kingdom. He compared their efforts to gaining profits and interest on wealth. He told them that those that only recruited a few converts would receive smaller stakes in the kingdom. Jesus offered nothing for those that refused to add converts to the kingdom (*Matthew 25:14-30*).

## 15. The International Kingdom

Jesus told his Apostles that his kingdom would begin in Judea, but that it would spread across the planet. That is not to say that the implementation of his kingdom would be easy. Jesus spoke both of positive and negative events occurring in connection with the coming kingdom. He first said that persons would come from everywhere on earth to reside in the Kingdom. Then, he predicted that their enemies would temporarily drive the "children of the kingdom" out (*Matthew 8:11-12*).

Jesus never hid the fact that his followers would suffer greatly for attempting to aid him in establishing his kingdom. He told them directly and without any sugarcoating that they could expect abuse from his enemies. He told them to expect arrest, trial and prison if they continued to stand by him (*Luke 21:12*).

Thus, none who followed Jesus could ever say that he had misled them or that he said that they would receive the rewards of the kingdom with ease.

Jesus was saying that the kingdom doctrine would draw many to it, but that they would suffer persecution. However, not all of those hearing Jesus understood his point.

Jesus said that his message would extend beyond Judea. He said that his followers would communicate his message to every nation so that the whole world would bear witness to his kingdom (*Matthew 24:14*).

However, he intended to have more than "witness" states. He envisioned them to be vassal states. Jesus declared that he would have power over every nation. In fact, Jesus told his Apostles that he would give friendly nations preferred treatment when he founded his kingdom and that he would punish those that opposed him with severity (*Matthew 25:31-46*).

Jesus again claimed the throne of Judea, but he likewise hammered home the point that his kingdom was international in nature. He told his followers in Judea that his task included informing persons of other lands of his kingdom (*Luke 4:43*).

Of course, the idea that the kingdom was international was a major theme in the *Gospels* from the beginning. In fact, the very first persons to recognize Jesus as a king were foreigners (*Matthew 2:1-3*).

Jesus relentlessly promoted the idea that his movement was international. On numerous occasions, he commented that persons would come from every direction to share in his kingdom (*Luke 13:29*).

Jesus had a definite plan for establishing a worldwide order. He stated that his kingdom would infiltrate the world like leaven hidden in meal. This was an indication that Jesus intended his followers to infiltrate the Roman Empire and transform it into a nation that followed his teachings (*Matthew 13:33*).

During his stories, Jesus left no doubt that his earthly kingdom would be a model for

God's heavenly one. He continued that God not only approved the establishment of the earthly kingdom, but also had ordered it (*Matthew 11:1-2*).

In the early days, Jesus told his followers not to concern themselves that their movement was small. He promised them that they would succeed (*Luke 12:32*).

The Judean religious leaders demanded that Jesus tell them when he intended to establish this international kingdom. Understanding that their question was a trap, Jesus refused to answer them directly. Instead, he told them that they would not know of the coming of the kingdom before hand (*Luke 17:20*).

## 16. Jesus Promotes Simon Peter

The *Gospels* mention Simon Peter first when they mention those that Jesus recruited as his Apostles (*Matthew 4:18*). This is no accident. Early on, Jesus granted Simon Peter a special place among the Apostles. In fact, Jesus promoted Simon Peter to the first place among the Apostles (*Matthew 10:2*).

Jesus revealed the promotion of Simon Peter in public because of the awareness Simon Peter displayed. It came about this way:

When Jesus took his message to Caesarea Philippi, which was the capital city of the region lorded over by Herod's half brother, Philip the Tetrarch. Caesarea Philippi was located in Northern Palestine and was about 105 miles from Jerusalem. While there, Jesus inquired of his Apostles about what the masses thought of him. The Apostles replied that some Judeans thought he had replaced John the Baptist, while others believed him to represent Elias or some other prophet (*Matthew 16:13-14*).

Then Jesus asked his Apostles who they thought he was and Simon Peter answered that he knew Jesus was the king sent to deliver Judea from its oppressors. Jesus was pleased that Simon Peter understood the mission on which Jesus was leading them. In fact, Simon Peter's answer made Jesus so happy that he promised to build his government on his astute Apostle. Jesus then promised to give Simon Peter the "keys of the kingdom." In other words, Jesus made Simon Peter the heir apparent to his earthly kingdom (*Matthew 16:15-19*).

The *Gospels* provide several examples of Simon Peter having the most important place among the Apostles:

(1) Jesus and his Apostles returned to his adopted home city of Capernaum. Capernaum was about 85 miles North of Jerusalem. While they were there, temple tax collectors approached Simon Peter. The tax collectors requested that Simon Peter inquire as to whether Jesus intended to pay the taxes they said he owed. The annual tax was required of every male citizen of at least twenty years of age. At that time, the Pharisees and Sadducees were embroiled in dispute as to whether the tax was mandatory or voluntary. Apparently, the tax collectors could not forcibly collect the tax, because they requested payment instead of demanding it.

When Simon Peter asked Jesus about the tax, Jesus maintained that he was not required to pay it. However, he ordered Simon Peter to pay it anyway. Jesus did not desire that his followers "stumble" into to thinking that they were not required to follow the secular law as well as religious law. Beyond that, Jesus did not want to give his enemies the opportunity to accuse him and his Apostles of being criminals or outlaws in any sense (*Matthew 17:24-27*).

It is obvious that the tax collectors came to Simon Peter because he held the highest rank among the Apostles.

(2) When the Apostles saw Jesus walking on the sea, the others waited for Simon Peter to call out to Jesus. In addition, Jesus took Simon Peter upon the sea with him (*Matthew 14:27-31*). Again, this indicates the esteem in which Jesus and the other Apostles held Simon Peter.

(3) When the Apostles did not understand a parable, Simon Peter asked Jesus to explain it (*Matthew 15:15*). Sometimes, Jesus became exasperated that the Apostles had difficulty understanding his message (*Matthew 15:16*). However, he always answered the questions posed to him by Simon Peter.

(4) Despite Jesus rebuking him, Simon Peter continued to attempt to get clarification as to the message Jesus proclaimed. For instance, Simon asked how often he should forgive someone who had wronged him. Jesus replied in a manner that indicated one should forgive endlessly (*Matthew 18:21-22*).

(5) When Jesus took several of his Apostles to a mountain to prove he was the Christ, Simon Peter spoke for the others (*Matthew 17:1-4*).

(6) Simon Peter represented the other Apostles when he inquired as to the reward they could expect for their service to Jesus (*Matthew 19:27*). (For the answer, see the next chapter.)

The examples above are powerful proof and undeniable proof that Simon Peter served as the lead Apostle.

## 17. Infighting among the Apostles

The *Gospels* point out that the 12 Apostles were not angelic souls. On the contrary, the Apostles were very, very human and they often revealed their most base desires.

The humanity of the Apostles reared its ugly head when they quibbled over which should have higher rank in the kingdom. Several believed that they rated a higher rank in the kingdom than the others. Several believed that when Jesus became king and they deserved to lord over the other Apostles.

Eventually, after arguing among themselves for some time, the Apostles went to Jesus and asked him who would be the greatest in the kingdom. Jesus told them that unless each of them became as children, that is, they put away all their vanity and egotism, not only would they not lead, they would not even enter into the kingdom. Further, he told them that those who became most like children would be the greatest in heaven (*Matthew 18:1-6; 19:14*).

In the above exchange, Jesus did more than just point out that it was vain of his Apostles to strive to be the greatest in his kingdom. He also made it clear that holding the office of Apostle did not ensure them any office in the kingdom. It is certain that Jesus was hinting that one of them would be with his enemies soon. Jesus also mentioned, in a hinting way, that one of the Apostles would soon hang (*Matthew 18:6*).

It is important to note that the answer Jesus gave indicated that he did not desire for his

Apostles to fight among themselves. However, it does indicate that the Apostles would not have equal positions in his kingdom.

As stated in the previous chapter, Simon Peter asked Jesus what reward the Apostles would receive for standing with him and Jesus revealed that he considered them the most important part of his monarchy. Jesus said that at the foundation of his kingdom his Apostles would sit on thrones near him and would play import roles in ruling Judea (*Matthew 19:27-28*).

However, Jesus cautioned them not to behave like leaders of secular governments, but to place their work as servants ahead of petty concerns. Finally, he challenged them to place themselves in the service of each other (*Luke 22:24-30*).

Not only did Jesus promise his Apostles great power, but also promised them great wealth. He promised them that he would repay their material sacrifice many times over. Thus, the Apostles stood to gain much for their commitment to Jesus (*Matthew 19:29-30*).

Jesus continued that he would reward those willing to make sacrifices for the sake of his kingdom more handsomely than they could ever imagine. However, he made it plain that the sacrifices would be great and that his followers might have to give up family, friends and worldly possessions in the service of the kingdom (*Luke 18:29-30*).

The Apostles continued to lust for greater power and influence even after Jesus had explained the situation to them. They continued to jockey for position with each other. On one instance, the mother of James and John asked Jesus to give her sons preferred offices in the kingdom. Jesus gladly confirmed the two as important members of his government, but he refused to commit to giving either a favored place among the leaders in the kingdom (*Matthew 20:20-23*).

When the other Apostles learned that James and John were lobbying for a preferred place in the kingdom, they were outraged. However, Jesus prevented a rupture between the members of his royal team by explaining to them that should not be like the leaders of other nations. He told them that they should all place the kingdom above their personal and political ambitions. He also told them that they should defer to one another (*Matthew 20:24-28*).

Even though Jesus did not rank his Apostles, beyond Simon Peter, a pecking order did develop. The *Gospels* do not directly list the Apostles by rank. However, we can assume a ranking system did exist because the Bible refers to Simon Peter as "the first" (*Matthew 10:2*). In addition, Jesus treated some Apostles as if they were more important than other Apostles were. For instance, he took Simon Peter, James and John up to a mountaintop and proved to them that he was the Christ (*Matthew 17:1-5*).

Finally, Jesus attempted to end the bickering between the Apostles by ordering them not to war with each other, but to present a unified front always (*Mark 9:50*).

## 18. Jesus Faces Opposition

When Jesus began his mission, he and John the Baptist were associated closely with each other. Therefore, when Jesus learned that Herod had ordered John the Baptist thrown into prison, he understood that he too was in imminent danger of arrest. In order to avoid detainment, Jesus went swiftly into Galilee (*Matthew 4:12; Mark 1:14*).

Galilee is a little more than 100 miles from Jerusalem and Jesus was certain that he would be safe there. 100 miles in those days was great enough a distance to allow a measure of anonymity. However, the message Jesus proclaimed was too provocative not to draw negative attention in a short time.

Jesus, as John the Baptist before him had, ran afoul of the traditional Judean religious leaders quickly. The Sadducees and Pharisees began their assault on him when they criticized Jesus and his Apostles because they did not always wash their hands before they ate (*Matthew 15:1-2*).

Jesus did not ignore his opponents. Instead, he defended his Apostles. He reacted to the criticism by pointing out that the precious "traditions" of the Sadducees and Pharisees were transgressions against the commandants of God. Jesus reminded Sadducees and Pharisees that the law commanded that all must honor their fathers and mothers. Yet, the self-proclaimed religious leaders of Judea routinely either ignored that commandment or denied it when applying their so-called traditions. Jesus continued that the Sadducees and Pharisees were hypocrites because they honored God verbally, to make themselves appear pious to others, but did not really believe in God's commandments (*Matthew 15:3-9*).

Jesus continued the discussion when he spoke to a large crowd and condemned the traditions of the Judean religious leaders. He told his audience that God does not consider one defiled by what he eats, but by what he says (*Matthew 15:10-11*).

After Jesus had finished, his Apostles came to him and told him that his words had angered the traditional Judean religious leaders who had heard them. Jesus told his followers not to worry because God would eventually uproot the Judean religious leaders. He continued that the Judean religious leaders should be let alone, because they were merely an example of the blind leading the bind and they would eventually fail of their own accord. Jesus then said that "evil thoughts, murders, adulteries, fornications, thefts, false witness (and) blasphemies..." filled his opponents (*Matthew 15:12-14, 19*).

Jesus asked his opponents what they had expected to see when they came to where he preached his message (*Matthew 11:8*). It was clear to Jesus that they would have opposed him regardless of the nature of his ministry.

Jesus continued that the opponents of the true kingdom had violently attacked it since the times of John the Baptist (*Matthew 11:12*).

Thus, Jesus made it clear that the attacks would not dissipate. He was correct; the attacks intensified.

The opponents of the kingdom message attempted to silence Jesus by making him afraid. They told him that if he did not leave Judea and stop proclaiming the true kingdom that Herod would kill him (*Luke 13:31*). Jesus had no doubt that Herod was more than willing to kill him just as he had John the Baptist. However, Jesus did not fear death. He told his opponents to go back to Herod and inform "that fox" pretending to be king that he would not abandon his mission (*Luke 13:32*).

Realizing that they could not intimidate Jesus, those opposing him decided that the only way to silence him was to "destroy" him. The Pharisees held a council where they decided to take him into custody and then devise a means to eliminate him (*Matthew 12: 14*).

However, Jesus learned of the plan to arrest him and he escaped before the religious leaders could capture him. In addition, Jesus ordered those near him not to do anything that would reveal his whereabouts to his opponents. Jesus understood that he could not avoid arrest indefinitely, but he needed to buy time to give his doctrine as wide a circulation as possible (*Matthew 12:15-18*).

Jesus had a point in delaying his arrest for as long as possible. As stated in Chapter 15, Jesus did not intend to be just the King of Judea. He desired that the Romans learn of him and spread his message throughout the entire world. He understood that the best way to spread his message in the short term was for him to remain free and preach as often as possible and to enlist as many converts as he could. Jesus left no doubt that his plan would ensure victory (*Matthew 12:19-21*).

Much to the chagrin to his opponents, Jesus was gaining followers throughout Judea in droves. More and more citizens of Judea accepted him as the rightful king of their land (*Matthew 12:23*).

The opponents of Jesus denied that he was the rightful king, but claimed that he was an agent of the Devil instead (*Matthew 12:24*). However, the verbal attacks on Jesus did not dissuade his followers.

Word of the exploits of Jesus spread across the countryside like a windblown wildfire and soon they came to the attention of Herod the Tetrarch. Upon hearing the news, Herod became distraught, because he believed that Jesus had replaced John as the chief opponent of the Herodian regime. Beyond that, Jesus had developed a much larger following than John had ever had. Herod realized that murdering John the Baptist had accomplished nothing (*Matthew 14:1-2*). Herod was no safer in his false rule than he had been before he decapitated the Baptist. Herod made no move against Jesus. However, he wished someone would eliminate his rival.

Of course, the traditional religious leaders of Judea would not simply allow Jesus to go forward with his mission without continuing to challenge him. The Pharisees and Sadducees put aside their differences temporarily and unified against Jesus. Some members of these factions came to Jesus and demanded he prove his truthfulness by giving them a sign from heaven. Jesus understood that his opponents were merely trying to trap him, so he refused to give a sign. However, he went farther than that. He told them that if they were not wicked hypocrites they could see the signs already before them (*Matthew 16:1-4*).

## 19. Jesus in Jerusalem

Jesus was ready to take the next step in his mission. He led his Apostils toward Jerusalem with the intent of his entering as the rightful King of Judea. A little over a mile from Jerusalem, they stopped at the Mount of Olives in the town of Bethphage. Jesus sent two of his Apostles to the nearby town of Bethany to get a donkey and a colt. His plan was to reveal himself as the true king by fulfilling a prophecy that the king would enter Jerusalem riding a donkey (*Matthew 21:1-5*).

The next morning, when Jesus departed for Jerusalem atop the donkey, a large crowd followed him proclaiming him as the true King of Judea. Of course, when Jesus entered the city, he made quite an impression and caused quite a stir. The entire city turned out to see Jesus and he convinced many that he was indeed the true King of Judea (*Matthew 21:9-10*).

The Pharisees and other Judean religious leaders in the great city were angry that so many proclaimed that Jesus was their king. When the Judean religious leaders verbally attacked Jesus, he responded that tax collectors and prostitutes would hold a higher place in his kingdom than they. He condemned them for rejecting John the Baptist while the tax collectors and prostitutes had accepted him (*Matthew 21:15, 31-32*).

Jesus continued that God would destroy the wicked and would give his blessings to others. He then told them that even though they rejected him, he would become the cornerstone of the kingdom and would deny them any part in it. He continued that he would make a place in the kingdom for Gentiles (*Matthew 21:41-45*).

When the Sadducees and Pharisees heard the speech Jesus made and realized that he placed them below the Gentiles, they became outraged and sought to capture him. However, they did not, because they feared that the huge crow would turn on them if they moved against Jesus (*Matthew 21:46*).

As stated earlier, the Pharisees and Sadducees had previously unified in their opposition to Jesus. Now, they held a meeting in which they decided to enlist the aid of the Herodians to in their attacks on Jesus (*Mark 3:6*). The Herodians were a small, but powerful political-religious organization dedicated to King Herod and the promotion of his dynasty (*Encyclopaedia Biblica: A Critical Dictionary of the Literary, Political and Religion History, the Archeology, Geography and Natural History of the Bible*).

Even though many of the Judean religious leaders were opposed to Herod generally, they saw Jesus as a greater threat than the false King of Judea. For their part, the Herodians supported Herod unconditionally and were more than willing to help in disposing of the rival claimant to the throne of Judea.

Understanding that Herod was loath to taking direct action against Jesus, these three parties worked to trap Jesus into making criminal utterances against Roman authority.

They found him in the midst of a large crowd and attempted to trick him into a crime. They asked him if Judeans should refuse to pay Imperial taxes. Jesus refused to allow them to bait him. He told his tempters that he knew what they were up to and then he told them that they should give to Creaser those things that were his and give to God those thing that was His. The answer was perfect. Jesus refused to oppose the power of Caesar; however, he did not concede any power that he claimed as his own. Those opposing Jesus knew they had failed in this attempt to trick Jesus and looked for other ways to attack him (*Matthew 22:15-22*).

However, before his opponents could continue, Jesus posed a question to them. He asked to what family they thought he belonged. They could not deny his heritage and they admitted that was of the house of David. Jesus then asked them how they could honestly deny his right to the throne when they admitted that the house of David was the legitimate ruling family of Judea. His logic was impeccable; if he was David's heir, he was the heir to the throne of Judea. His opponents agreed that Jesus was the heir to the throne of David, but they would not concede his right to rule. Thus, they could not continue the argument, so they left the scene quietly (*Matthew 22:41-46*).

Jesus spoke to a large crowd and told them that they should observe those laws and customs that the Sadducees and Pharisees told them to observe. However, he told them not to do as the Sadducees and Pharisees did. He continued that the Sadducees and Pharisees only gave lip service to the ancient laws and customs of Judea (*Matthew 23:1-3*).

Jesus then went into detail as to why his audience should not follow the traditional Judean religious leaders. He told those listening what they already knew. Jesus said that the Sadducees and Pharisees placed heavy burdens on them, but would not follow their own rules. Jesus continued that the Sadducees and Pharisees wanted the best of the material things and the respect of average citizens. However, they were willing to nothing to earn those things or that respect (*Matthew 23:4-12*). The crowd roared with approval at what Jesus said to them.

Then Jesus broke into a long tirade condemning the traditional religious leaders as liars and hypocrites. He called them venomous serpents and again promised to exclude them from entering his kingdom (*Matthew 23:13-36*).

Next, Jesus spoke of his capital, Jerusalem, and said that because the citizens there would eventually reject him, its throne would remain empty until they repented and specifically asked him to accept it (*Matthew 23: 37-39*).

As time went along, the Judean religious leaders realized that they could not trap Jesus and they went after the Apostles. After having many unsuccessful disputes with the Apostles, the traditional religious leaders asked Jesus to silence his followers. Jesus refused. On the contrary, he told the religious leaders that no power on earth could silence his followers (*Luke 19:39-40*).

## 20. Jesus Accused of Crimes

Of course, those opposing Jesus could not allow him to keep denouncing them. Thus, they had to remove him from the scene. However, they could not very well do away with him without accusing him of violations of Judean religious or Roman secular law, or both. During the time Jesus promoted the coming kingdom, his opponents accused him of various crimes. Below is a short list of the accusations made against Jesus.

Judean religious leaders accused Jesus of violating Judean religious law by healing sick and infirmed citizens on the Sabbath. Jesus responded that if a shepherd found one of his sheep in a pit on the Sabbath, he would certainly pull it out. Therefore, Jesus contended that it was as lawful for him to heal Judeans on the Sabbath as it was for a shepherd to pull a sheep out of as pit on the Sabbath (*Matthew 12:10-11*). Thus, Jesus pointed out that the Judean religious leaders did not really understand their own laws.

His opponents accused Jesus of being gluttonous and of being a drunkard. They also accused him of consorting with befriending criminals, tax collectors and persons of ill repute (*Matthew 11:19, 9:10, Luke 7:34*). The first charges were unfounded. Jesus had never displayed gluttony or lack of temperance with alcoholic beverages. Of course, eating and drinking were not crimes in any regard. As to befriending "sinners", Jesus never denied it. In fact, seeking out those who needed him and attending to them was a point of emphasis with him. Beyond that, Matthew, one of the Apostles, had been a tax collector.

Jesus received heavy rebuke from Judean leaders for throwing the moneychangers out of the temple (*Matthew 21:12-13*). However, this was clearly not a crime. In fact, Judean laws forbid such activity in the temple in the first place. Thus, when he threw the moneychangers out, he enforced the law while his opponents violated the law by allowing it.

Those opposing Jesus contended that he acted without legal authority when he declared he was the King of Judea (*Matthew 21:23*). However, the Judean leaders admitted Jesus was of the House of David. Thus, by their own testimony they proved that Jesus did have legal authority based on his undeniable birthright as the heir to the throne of Judea.

Another charge opponents made was that Jesus had threatened to destroy the temple (*Matthew 26:61*). Of course, Jesus had made remarks concerning the temple as a way of foretelling the resurrection, but he never threatened to destroy it. In fact, he talked of rebuilding it (*John 2:19*).

The Judean religious leaders also accused Jesus of employing demons to cast out demons. Jesus pointed out that the contention was ludicrous and that it was impossible to use demons to cast themselves, or other demons, out (*Mark 3:22-26*).

The Judean religious leaders continued to claim that Jesus and his followers were in violation of religious law because of their unsanitary eating habits. Jesus countered them by pointing that the blasphemous utterances of his opponents were far more corrupting than a little dirt on the Apostles' hands (*Matthew 15:3-9*).

Secular crimes that opponents accused Jesus of committing included "perverting the nation" and stirring up the Judeans against the king; declaring that he was the true King of Judea and opposing paying Roman taxes (*Luke 23:2-5*). Jesus had had always instructed his followers to pay their taxes. In fact, he had paid taxes that he did not legally owe (*Matthew 22:17-21*). He never denied that he was the true King of Judea, which was true. Therefore, it was not a crime. Of course, if he were the true king he was not "perverting" or stirring up anybody or anything.

All and all, the charges made against Jesus were a sorry lot. The silly, ridiculous and politically motivated testimony against Jesus was so thin that even the Romans found them unworthy of serious consideration. Yet, the Judean religious leaders continued to spout them all the way until – and after – Jesus expired upon the cross.

## 21. Judas Betrays Jesus

Jesus utilized his Apostles in the same way the American President utilizes Cabinet secretaries and bureaucrats. Jesus afforded each of the Apostles specific duties to perform and then allowed them the flexibility to carry out those tasks with minimal supervision. Jesus made Judas Iscariot treasurer in his government. Judas oversaw all the funds earmarked for use by Jesus and his Apostles. It is likely that Judas had training as an accountant. However, the *Gospels* do not state this directly. What the *Gospels* do indicate is that Judas was a thief (*John 12:6*).

Judas Iscariot evidently dipped into the moneybox until it was nearly empty. Then he found himself struggling to find a way to replenish it before someone discovered his thefts.

Judas Iscariot made his first effort to cover his crime when he complained because Mary intended to treat Jesus with a very expensive ointment. He suggested that Jesus allow him to sell the ointment and to use the funds in the aid of the poor instead. Of course, Judas Iscariot had no intention to give the money from the sell to the poor. Instead, he intended to use the funds for his own purposes. Jesus rejected the suggestion of Judas Iscariot curtly and instructed Mary to continue treating him (*John 12:3-8*).

The fact that he requested approval to sell the ointment indicates that Judas Iscariot was desperate to find a means to cover pervious thefts. At this point, had Judas Iscariot confessed his crimes and promised to reform and repent, Jesus would have forgiven him. However, Judas was not yet ready to take responsibility for his actions.

When Jesus refused the request, Judas Iscariot found his situation even more desperate than before. He devised another plan to cover his crimes. He was also, no doubt, enraged that Jesus had thwarted his plan to cover up his crime and to solve his money problems temporarily. Beyond that, Judas Iscariot doubtlessly desired to punish Christ for complicating his plans. The ever-devious Judas Iscariot soon found a way to do both.

Shortly before the Passover, the religious leaders of Judea assembled in the palace of the High Priest, Caiaphas. The purpose of the meeting was to devise to best method to capture and eliminate Jesus without causing a stir among the lower classes of Judea. The Judean religious leaders were especially wary of doing away with Jesus during the Passover feast (*Matthew 26:3-5*).

During the meeting of the Judean religious leaders, Judas Iscariot came before them, identified himself and inquired what they would pay him to deliver Jesus to them. The religious leaders were happy to have assistance from inside the inner circle of Jesus. With little debate, they offered Judas Iscariot the hefty sum of thirty pieces of silver to help them and he accepted without negotiating. From that point onward, Judas Iscariot sought a time and place to put Jesus into the hands of his enemies without arousing a crowd and causing an uproar (*Matthew 26:14-16*).

Jesus understood that Judas Iscariot intended to betray him. During his last meal with his Apostles Jesus informed them that one of them would soon deliver him to his enemies. Oddly, all the Apostles feared that they might be the betrayer. Each of them inquired as to the identity of the traitor. Jesus did not answer each of them directly, but told them to watch for a sign to reveal the betrayer. However, when Judas Iscariot asked Jesus if he was the betrayer, Jesus whispered an answer to him in the affinitive (*Matthew 26:20-25*).

Jesus then told Judas Iscariot to do what he was about to do quickly. Oddly, even though Jesus had given them the sign to watch for, the other Apostles did not realize the reason Jesus spoke to Judas Iscariot personally. They assumed that Jesus was ordering Judas to take funds and either make some necessary purchase, or give some of it to the poor (*John 13:25-29*).

Judas Iscariot departed and after their meal, Jesus and his other Apostles went to a place called the Brook of Cedron (now usually spelled Kidron). The Brook of Cedron was in a ravine in eastern Jerusalem between the present Temple Mound and the Mount of Olives. Jesus often rested in the lush, green garden there (*John 18:1*).

Judas Iscariot knew that Jesus would take repose in the garden, so when he assembled his large contingent of armed men to capture

Jesus, he knew exactly where to lead them (*John 18:2*).

Judas Iscariot doubtlessly believed the Brook of Cedron was the perfect place to capture Jesus. Being in a ravine, there was no way Jesus could escape. Beyond that, the Brook of Cedron was secluded and few would be around to prevent the capture.

When Judas Iscariot and his horde arrived, Jesus made no effort to escape or to hide his identity. However, not all his Apostles were as passive as Jesus was. Simon Peter attempted to fight back. The chief Apostle slashed at and slightly wounded one would-be abductor called Malchus. However, Jesus stopped Simon Peter before the situation got out of hand. He submitted to his arrest without further incident (*John 18:3-14*).

Only after Judas Iscariot delivered Jesus that did he become aware that his employers intended to kill Jesus. When Judas learned the judges of the Sanhedrin intended to condemn Jesus to death he realized that plan would not work out the way he thought. He had expected the Sanhedrin to discredit Jesus, but not to pursue his execution. Judas Iscariot knew that the other Apostles would ostracize him when they learned that he had received payment to betray Jesus. He attempted to salvage his position among the other Apostles by returning the bribe the Judean religious leaders had given him. He thought doing so would prove him innocent in his fellow Apostles' eyes. He told the Judean religious leaders that he had reconsidered and he now thought Jesus was innocent. The religious leaders told Judas Iscariot that his present opinion did not matter. They said that he had earned the "blood money" and that he should keep it (*Matthew 27:3-4*).

Knowing his plan had exploded, Judas Iscariot felt trapped. His plan to cover his crimes had failed and he had lost his place among the Apostles. Beyond that, the Judean religious leaders and the people of Judea would see him as a betrayer and would treat him as an outcast.

Thus, Judas Iscariot saw no other option except to commit suicide. He left the bribe money with the religious leaders, found a tree and hanged himself from it (*Matthew 27:5*).

The Judean religious leaders could not legally put the blood money Judas Iscariot had left with them into the treasury. They had a meeting on the subject in which they decided to use the blood money to purchase a cemetery to bury the indigent (*Matthew 27:6-10*). Therefore, ironically, Judas Iscariot helped the poor after all.

## 22. Why Judas Betrayed Jesus

For centuries, historians, biblical scholars and others have questioned why Judas Iscariot betrayed Jesus and then committed suicide afterward. In this chapter, the author takes a few words to explore the interesting topic of the motivations of Judas Iscariot.

Jesus gave Judas Iscariot the very important task of controlling the ministry cashbox. Some contend that Jesus already knew the evil nature of Judas Iscariot when they first met and that Jesus utilized this knowledge to cause Judas to betray him. Others contend that Jesus gave Judas Iscariot the task based on qualifications alone. Regardless as to why Jesus tasked Judas Iscariot to watch over the cashbox, Judas took advantage of the situation and stole from it.

It is very likely that Jesus knew early on that Judas Iscariot was a thief and that he put pressure on his criminal Apostle without actually exposing him. Fearing imminent exposure, and needing to find a means to cover his crimes, the desperate and panicking Apostle sold Jesus to his enemies.

The *Gospels* opine as to why Judas Iscariot betrayed Jesus. In one passage, John indicates that Judas Iscariot was "a devil" (*John 6:70-71*). In another passage, Luke stated, "Satan entered into Judas" (*Luke 22:3-6*). The authors of those two statements may have meant that a literal demon possessed Judas Iscariot or, more likely, they may have meant that Judas Iscariot simply lacked moral character. Judas Iscariot reveals his lack of character by that fact that he initiated contact with the Judean religious leaders and offered to aid them (*Matthew 26:14-16*). This indicates that Judas Iscariot did not succumb to temptation and was not tricked or blackmailed by the Judean religious leaders, but was the driving force behind the plot.

There are other hints as to why Judas Iscariot chose to steal from Jesus and then to betray him. As mentioned earlier, Judas Iscariot was the only of the 12 original Apostles who did not hail from Galilee. This certainly made him feel as if he were an outsider and caused him to be alienated from the others. He, no doubt, had a much easier time stealing from those towards which he no feelings of affinity or friendship. Again, since he had no personal or emotional attachment to Jesus or the other Apostles, he found little difficulty with betraying his master.

Greed is a powerful emotion and Judas Iscariot was certainly greedy. He stole from the moneybox and used the money for his own purposes. Ambition is another powerful emotion and as we have seen, the Apostles were ambitious. Judas Iscariot saw his ambitions damaged when Jesus refused to accept council from him. This, no doubt, infuriated the criminal Apostle. Beyond that, Judas Iscariot understood that if Jesus and the Apostles discovered his crimes, not only would he not have a preferred place in the kingdom, he would likely no leadership role in the kingdom at all.

As to why Judas Iscariot took his own life, the answer is simpler than what one might imagine. Since Judas Iscariot did not have an emotional attachment to Jesus or the other Apostles, it is unlikely that he committed suicide out of a sense of guilt. On the contrary, he designed his plot to cover his crimes. When Judas Iscariot finally realized that his plan had failed and that he was certain to be exposed, his cowardice bubbled to the surface and his fear overcame him. Judas was out of plans; he was out of deceptions. Thus, he took the coward's way out and hung himself.

## 23. Jesus Executed

Jesus and his Apostles made their way to Jerusalem for what they all knew would be a showdown. However, the Apostles did not understand the true purpose of their march into the great city. They thought that Jesus intended to overthrow Herod and to announce the establishment of his government (*Luke 19-11*).

Jesus attempted to reveal his true intentions by telling his Apostles a story. This story was about a king rejected by his subjects who left for a period and then returned. When this king returned, he rewarded his followers who had kept their word and prepared the way for his return. Then, he punished those who had not done anything to aid his return (*Luke 19: 12-27*).

Of course, Jesus was telling his Apostles that he was NOT on the verge of establishing his kingdom, but that he was leaving them soon. From what we know of what happened next, it is clear that even this story did not make the Apostles understand what was about to happen in Jerusalem. Jesus had been preparing his Apostles for his pending arrest; however, they did not understand that Jesus was to die no matter how direct he was in his explanation. They believed that he would not die because he promised them that they would be in the kingdom together with him (*Matthew 26:2, 29*).

While Jesus was preparing those Apostles who were with him for his arrest, Judas Iscariot came to him. As stated earlier, just behind Judas Iscariot, a heavily armed band under the command of the religious leaders of Judea came to arrest Jesus. However, those who intended to capture Jesus did not know him personally and could not tell him from those with him. Judas Iscariot had previously told his comrades that they should lay hold of the one that he kissed (*Matthew 26:47-48*).

Judas greeted Jesus and then kissed him. Jesus knew what was happening and asked Judas, "Why are you here?" Judas did not reply. Instead, the armed men took hold of Jesus (*Matthew 26:49-50*).

Again, as stated in the previous chapter, Simon Peter, who believed it was his task to protect Jesus, drew his sword, struck and injured one of the armed men attempting to abduct Jesus (*Matthew 26:51*).

Jesus ordered Simon Peter to put away his sword and not to resist the men arresting him. Then Jesus explained that the arrest was necessary to fulfill his mission (*Matthew 26:52-54*).

Then, Jesus turned to the leaders of those arresting him and implied they were cowards when he asked them why they came for him as thieves in the night when they could have arrested him on any of the many times he had spoken before them in the temple. The arresters did not respond to him (*Matthew 26:55*). The use of the term "thieves" certainly indicated that he knew why Judas Iscariot had betrayed him.

When the armed band bound Jesus, his Apostles (including Simon Peter, who had initially displayed bravely) lost their nerve and ran away (*Matthew 26:56*).

The abductors took Jesus before Annas. Annas was the father of Caiaphas, the High Priest. Annas had no authority to act, so he ordered Jesus taken directly to stand trial before the Sanhedrin over which Caiaphas presided (*Matthew 26:57; John 18:13*).

The court was stacked against Jesus, but his accusers had no real evidence that he had committed any crime whatever. Since they had no legitimate evidence by which to condemn Jesus, they sought to manufacture some (*Matthew 26:59-60*). (See Chapter 20)

Of course, if this evidence had been true, Jesus would have been in violation of both Judean and – more importantly – Roman law. Throughout the testimony against him, Jesus remained silent. High Priest Caiaphas finally asked Jesus if he had any defense to the testimony against him and Jesus did not respond. Then the High Priest asked Jesus directly if he claimed the throne of Judea. Jesus replied that the trial had proven that he was the true king. Then, Jesus declared that he would "sit on the right hand of power" (*Matthew 26:62-64*).

The reply outraged the High Priest. In fact, he became so angry that he tore his clothes. After several moments, the High Priest finally regained enough composure to declare that Jesus was guilty of blasphemy and that no further testimony was necessary. Caiaphas then turned to the court and asked what punishment Jesus deserved. The court rendered a verdict of death. At that point, members of the court physically attacked Jesus. They spit on, slapped and kicked the rightful king (*Matthew 26: 65-67*). Jesus made no defense against his attackers.

Even though the Sanhedrin had condemned Jesus to suffer death, it did not have the legal authority to carry out the sentence. The morning after the Sanhedrin condemned Jesus; the religious leaders delivered him to Roman authorities for an Imperial trial (*Matthew 27:1-2*).

Pontius Pilate served as Roman Governor of Judea from 26 AD to 36 AD. While the Roman Emperor recognized Herod as king of a portion of Judea, he ordered Pilate to protect Roman interests there. Therefore, Pilate had almost unlimited power and could veto any decree Herod issued (*Josephus Flavius, Jewish Antiquities*).

Pilate was clearly loath to entangle the Empire in what he saw as a minor religious squabble confined to local Jewish sects. When he learned that Jesus was a citizen of Galilee, Pilate saw an opportunity to shift the responsibility for the matter back to Judean authorities. He ordered the prisoner delivered to Herod for disposition.

Herod was happy that the Judean religious leaders had laid hold of Jesus. However, he feared executing him. Herod had caused a major uproar among his subjects when he made a martyr out of John the Baptist and he did not desire to repeat that mistake again. Therefore, Herod refused to judge his rival. Instead, Herod had Jesus beaten severely and then taken back to Pilate for a Roman trial (*Luke 23:6-11*).

Since Herod refused to let him off the hook, Pilate felt he had little choice except to put Jesus on trial. Pilate feared that if he did not act, the Judeans would see him as weak and indecisive and that he would lose the respect of his subjects. Beyond that, if he released Jesus without a trial, the squabble between the warring Judean sects would continue and it might lead to serious consequences.

Pilate certainly saw the irony in the fact that the figurehead king had found a way to control the situation and the Roman Governor – the most powerful person in all Judea – had no choice but to do the bidding of King Herod.

A restless and bored Pilate heard the testimony of the accusers. The opponents of Jesus repeated their former accusations.

Throughout the testimony of the accusers, Jesus remained silent. Finally, Pilate became exasperated and encouraged Jesus to offer a defense. He asked Jesus if he were the rightful King of Judea. At this point Jesus spoke up and asked if Pilate was making the accusation or if the Judean religious leaders were making the charge. The question annoyed Pilate. The Governor angrily demanded an answer and then he reminded Jesus that it was the

Judeans, not the Romans, making the accusations (*John 18:34-35*).

Jesus answered that his kingdom was not of the current time and that is why his Apostles and other Disciples did not fight to prevent his arrest. Jesus then repeated that his kingdom was of a future time (*John 18:36*).

The answer did not satisfy Pilate. He desired to clarify if Jesus claimed Judea as his realm. Pilate again asked if Jesus was a king. Jesus then admitted that he was born a king and that was the purpose of his entire life. Jesus also implied that the trial was itself proof that he was the true King of Judea (*John 18:37*).

The lack of defense offered by Jesus chagrined Pilate. Yet, the evidence against the prisoner was not great enough to convict him of any crime outright (*Matthew 27:12-14*).

Pilate was unwilling to admit that Jesus was correct in his contention that he was a king, but the Governor was still inclined to acquit him (*John 18:38*). However, the Judean religious leaders were relentless in their lobbying for a conviction and Pilate lacked the courage to risk his position by outraging such a loud and powerful clique. In addition, Herod desired Pilate to eliminate Jesus for him.

Pilate was in a bind. Therefore, the Governor kept Jesus in custody without actually finding him guilty of a crime until he could decide how to proceed. Pilate soon found a way out of his dilemma, or so he thought.

The Passover feast was upon Judea and Pilate believed he could increase his popularity if he released a "notable" Judean prisoner. Pilate decided to let the people of Jerusalem chose between two prisoners and have the most popular prisoner released to them (*Matthew 27:15*).

The two prisoners Pilate allowed the Judeans to choose from were Jesus and a notorious revolutionary and murderer who belonged to the Zealot sect named Barabbas (*Matthew 27:16-17*).

Pilate chose Jesus as one of the two because he believed that there was no evidence that Jesus had broken any Roman law (*Matthew 27:18-19*). On the other hand, Barabbas had become infamous by making war on the Romans. However, Pilate was a crafty politician. He believed his offer to parole such an anti-Roman rebel would endear him to the Judeans.

The Judean religious leaders had no love for either of the revolutionaries, but they viewed Jesus as more dangerous to them than Barabbas. Therefore, they encouraged the thousands on hand to vote for the murderer (*Matthew 27:20*).

The total number who took part in the vote is unknown, but it was definitely in the thousands – perhaps in the tens or even hundreds of thousands. In the first Century AD, somewhere between 20,000 and 50,000 persons resided in Jerusalem on a permanent basis. However, during festivals such as Passover, that number ballooned to somewhere between 80,000 and 125,000. Of course, most of the 60,000 to 75,000 tourists were present at the spectacle and they were free to take part in the vote (*Josephus Flavius, Jewish Antiquities*).

After allowing the supporters of both the candidates to stir up the crowd in favor of their choice for a brief time, Pilate asked which they wished him to release. A large majority of the crowd responded with a loud, "BARABBAS!" (*Matthew 27:21*).

Pilate acted surprised by the decision of the crowd. Whether he really was surprised or not, he still had no stomach for executing Jesus. Neither was Pilate keen on releasing the man Barabbas whom had already killed several Roman soldiers.

Pilate attempted to salvage a situation of which he was quickly losing control. He asked the crowd what they would have him do with Jesus. He hoped, no doubt, that they would ask for his release. Again, prompted by the Judean religious leaders, the bloodthirsty mob roared hoarsely, "CRUCIFY HIM!" (*Matthew 27:22*).

Not yet ready to concede to the mob rule he had created, Pilate reasoned with the crowd. Pilate attempted to convince the teeming mass that Jesus was innocent of any crime. However, the majority refused to listen to him; they demanded blood (*Matthew 27:23*).

Pilate realized that he could not regain control of the mob, so he decided to distance himself from it *and* to distance himself from the execution of Jesus. He told the mob that he would allow the execution of Jesus, but that the death of their king would be on their heads.

The crowd displayed no fear of carrying blame for the execution of Jesus (*Matthew 27:24-25*).

The mob had called all of Pilate's bluffs and he had no choice except to release a dangerous murderer and to execute an innocent man. Pilate reluctantly ordered the Zealot Barabbas turned over to the crowd and then he ordered Jesus publicly beaten and then turned over to the Roman soldiers that made up the execution squad (*Matthew 27:26*).

The execution squad took custody of Jesus and abused him for several hours in the most brutal way they could manage. They also mockingly declared that he was the "King of Judea" (*Matthew 27:27-31*).

Pilate was unhappy that he had been "forced" to execute Jesus. In order to exact some degree of revenge against the religious leaders of Judea and King Herod, the Imperial Governor ordered that soldiers to affix a placard at the top of the cross. He further ordered them to write "THIS IS JESUS THE KING OF THE JEWS." in Latin, Greek and Hebrew on the placard so that everyone literate person who saw the message would understand it, regardless of which language he spoke. Of course, the placard offended the religious leaders of Judea and they asked Pilate to alter or remove it. However, Pilate flatly refused to do so (*Matthew 27:37; Luke 23:28; John 19:27*).

The Roman soldiers nailed Jesus to a cross and hoisted him upon it for everyone to see. Jesus was dead in a few hours from his torturous ordeal (*Matthew 27:50*).

## 24. Reaction to the Execution

As one might imagine, the reaction to the execution of Jesus was different depending upon the faction to which one belonged. Below is a look at the reactions of the major players in the crucifixion of Jesus.

### Pontius Pilate

Pilate felt good about the outcome. He gained a measure of what he wanted from the execution of the innocent Jesus. Herod had disliked Pilate and the restraints the Governor put on his rule. However, Pilate's willingness to dispose of a claimant to the throne engendered gratefulness from Herod and after that, the king was more willing to accept the direction of the Imperial Governor. (*Luke 23:12*).

Beyond that, Pilate believed that he had avoided the possibility of a Judean revolt that he feared would occur if he went against the will of Herod and the Judean religious leaders and left Jesus alive. In addition, Pilate felt that the citizens of Judea would more easily bend to his will now that he had allowed them to vote to commute the sentence of a condemned criminal.

### Herod

Herod was happy indeed that Pilate had done away with his rival for him. Now with Jesus dead, the bothersome rumors of a coming king would finally end. In addition, there would be no more irritating claims that his marriage was illegal.

Herod did not mind ceding even more authority to the Romans as long as he maintained the trappings of his monarchy and he did not have to endure the burden of anyone proclaiming a true king was in his midst.

## The Judean Religious Leaders

The Judean religious leaders felt a burden lifted from them as well. With the kingdom movement destroyed, they were now free to resume their internal squabbling and petty battling for control of the hearts and souls of the Judean people. Beyond that, they believed that they would gain favor from Herod because of their willingness to do his bidding.

## The Apostles

As for the Apostles, they were devastated at first. Their leader's lifeless body resided in a cold, dark tomb (*Matthew 27:60*). They were without a clear plan as to what to do next (*Mark 16:14*). Beyond that, they had to live with the fact that one of them had delivered Jesus to his enemies and the other eleven had abandoned their master.

The one universal belief that these groups shared on the hour that Jesus died was that the kingdom ministry was finished. Of course, they were all wrong.

## 25. The Apostles Afterward

No book of this sort would be complete without looking at the activities of the men whom Jesus chose to be leaders in his kingdom after the Crucifixion. This chapter does that, albeit very briefly. We can learn a great deal about the politics of the times in which Jesus – and those times immediately after his execution – lived simply by learning a bit about those that followed Jesus.

After Jesus died upon the cross, the eleven living Apostles – along with Matthias, whom they elected from 120 lesser Disciples to replace Judas Iscariot (*Acts 1:15-27*) – endeavored to spread the message of the kingdom throughout the entire world.

The men mentioned here – along with a former persecutor of Christians, Paul – are responsible for the early growth of the faith.

One thing is important to remember here. It is not always possible to identify exact dates, or places, or even names when we are dealing with First Century events. However, enough information exists that we can provide a fair, unbiased sketch of the Apostles without relying on pure supposition or mere guesses.

We have more information about some Apostles than we do others. Therefore, some of these sketches are somewhat longer than others are. The length a given sketch does not necessarily indicate the importance of a given Apostle, however.

# Simon Peter

Simon Peter abandoned Jesus shortly after Christ's arrest (*Matthew 26:74*). However, he soon found his faith again and recommitted himself to the cause of Christianity. He resumed his leading role in preaching the kingdom message (*Mark 16:7*).

Shortly after the Romans crucified Jesus, the Apostles agreed to spread out across the world so that everyone could hear the message of the coming kingdom. Because he was the most important Apostle, it fell to Simon Peter to spread the message in the capital of the world. Thus, Simon Peter went to Rome and established the Christian Church there. In fact, according to the Roman Catholic Church, he became the first Pope (Birks, H. A., *Studies in the life and character of St. Peter*).

Simon Peter successfully promoted Christianity and brought thousands of Romans into the faith. However, he was often embroiled in public controversies and disputes with the practitioners of the official Roman religion. The corpulent Emperor Nero despised and feared Christianity. He believed that it was a danger to both the Roman faith and to his political power. The Emperor's fear rested largely on the fact that while Simon Peter reached out to everyone, it was the poor and disenfranchised that most readily received his message.

After many of his attempts to persecute the Christians out of existence failed, Nero finally decided that eliminating Simon Peter was the only way to destroy Christianity, so he ordered Peter arrested and crucified in 64 AD.

## Andrew

After the crucifixion of Jesus, instead of going to Rome with Peter, Andrew went to Asia Minor and Greece. After working to establish Christianity in the eastern portions of the Roman Empire for many years, Roman authorities took Andrew into custody and executed him in 60 AD.

## James the Greater

After the Crucifixion, James the Greater traveled across Rome's western frontier and preached the news of the coming kingdom in the far reaches of the Roman frontier. He traveled as far away as Spain preaching the message. However, after several years, James the Greater returned to Judea.

Christianity gained ground in Judea in the years after the crucifixion of Jesus. This led Judean religious leaders to petition the ruler of Judea, Herod Agrippa I (the grandson of Herod the Great) to suppress what they called the kingdom cult. Herod Agrippa pandered to the Judean religious leaders at every opportunity; therefore, he was more than willing to persecute the Christians.

As stated earlier, James the Greater was loud in his proclamations of the kingdom and Herod Agrippa I decided to make him the first Christian leader punished. As was the case with all those crucified, James the Greater refused to curtail his preaching in order to save his life. After exploring several ways to remove his nemesis, Herod Agrippa I finally ordered

James the Greater executed during Passover in 44 AD.

### John

After the Romans crucified Jesus, John continued to spread the good news of the coming kingdom until Herod Agrippa I embarked upon the savage persecution of Christians. After that, around 48 AD, John traveled to Asia Minor and spread the doctrine of the coming kingdom, especially at Ephesus. Ephesus was a Greek city located in present-day Turkey and the citizens there readily accepted Christianity.

John returned to Jerusalem for the Apostolic Council in 51 AD, but he did not remain there for very long. Soon after the Apostolic Council ended, John returned to Asia Minor and continued his work. Beyond his preaching, John also authored several religious books.

John did not suffer martyrdom. On the contrary, John lived deep into old age and did not die until about 100 AD.

### Philip

Sometime after the martyrdom of Jesus, the Apostle Philip began spreading the kingdom message at Caesarea, which is about 60 miles north of Jerusalem, then at Ephesus and finally at another Greek city in present-day Turkey called Hieropolis. Philip died in Hieropolis and his congregation buried his remains there. However, the date of his death is uncertain. There is no hard evidence that Philip suffered a martyr's death, but the tradition among the Christians is that he did.

## Bartholomew

After the Romans hoisted Jesus upon a cross, and the Apostles spread out across the earth preaching the news of the coming kingdom, Bartholomew traveled across "India" and some of the places he visited included Mesopotamia, Persia, Egypt, Armenia, Laconia, Phrygia, and towns and villages bordering the Black Sea.

Bartholomew finally settled in present-day Albania at Albanopolis (also called Zgerdhesh) and used it as a base of operation. The number of those Bartholomew converted to Christianity there was so great as to threaten the Armenian monarchy. Armenian authorities viewed Bartholomew and his faith to be revolutionary in nature. They arrested and publicly executed him in Albanopolis. It appears that Bartholomew's ordeal was particularly brutal. There are accounts that indicate that the Armenians bound, whipped, crucified and then, beheaded him.

## Thomas Didymus

After Thomas Didymus saw the arisen Jesus, he reaffirmed his faith and continued his mission (*John 20:28*).

Thomas received an assignment to go to India; however, he balked at first. Then, after a time Thomas Didymus fulfilled his commission and preached the doctrine of the coming kingdom at Andrapolis and Syriac Mazdai (in or near present-day India), then later in Afghanistan, the Punjab, and elsewhere.

Thomas Didymus ran up against several monarchs. He was condemned to death by several of them. Yet, he converted others. The most important monarch Thomas converted was the king Gondophares.

After surviving several attempts to martyr Thomas Didymus, the ruling monarch finally ordered his execution at Mylapore, India sometime after 46 AD.

Thomas Didymus is an important figure in *Gnostic* literature. The *Gnostic* work *The Acts of Thomas* helped shape that movement. There also exists a fragment called *The Gospel of Thomas*, which also follows the basic Gnostic view of the world. However, there is nothing in the *Gnostic* literature concerning Thomas Didymus that a historian can use. The author of *The Acts of Thomas* penned the book no earlier than the 5th Century AD and perhaps long after that.

## Matthew the Tax Collector

We know little of what Matthew did after the Romans executed Jesus. We do know that Matthew preached the word of the coming kingdom in Judea, Egypt, Persia, Greece, Syria and elsewhere.

There is no hard evidence to prove that Matthew suffered a martyr's death. At least one report states that he was not martyred. However, other reports indicate that he was stoned, burned, crucified or done to death in some other way. The events of his later life are so sketchy that it is impossible to determine with any kind of certainty that he was martyred.

## James the Lesser

After Jesus was executed, James the Lesser remained in Jerusalem and became the Bishop there. James the Lesser was in the forefront to relieve Gentiles of the burden of dietary laws and circumcision. These changes to Judean standards made it much easier to bring Gentiles into the Church. The easing of Judean religious law eventually led to Christianity becoming a religion populated by mostly Gentiles. However, James continued to follow the Judean standard and he never formally declared Judean religious law replaced by anything else.

James the Lesser went beyond simply following Judean religious law, however. He refused to consume alcohol or meat. Neither did James the Lesser shave, cut his hair or bathe.

Today's Bible contains a book authored by James the Lesser. The book indicates that he was less volatile and gentler than other Apostles were. His calm demeanor apparently allowed James the Lesser to continue to build and increase the Christian Church in Jerusalem for a generation.

James the Lesser remained Bishop of Jerusalem until at least 58 AD. However, even a man as meek as James the Lesser could not avoid persecution for all time. Opponents of Christianity finally decided that James the

Lesser had to be silenced and he suffered a martyr's death.

### Jude (Thaddaeus Lebbaeus, Judas)

We know virtually nothing of Jude after the execution of Jesus. We do know that Jude was a family man and that he had children and grandchildren.

Jude most likely remained in Jerusalem and aided his brother with building Christianity there over the next generation. However, we cannot be certain of that. There is no evidence that Jude suffered martyrdom. Yet, it only makes sense that he was martyred, if for no other reason than his close identification with his brother.

### Simon the Canaanite

Simon the Canaanite continued to spread the kingdom message after The Romans executed Jesus. However, it is unclear as to where he preached. He is associated with the Church in Jerusalem, but he is also associated with churches elsewhere as well. Greek, Egyptian, Ethiopian, Samarian, British, Spanish, Iranian and Russian sources all list him as preaching among them. While it is practically impossible that Simon the Canaanite could have preached in all those places, his constant mention is proof enough that he was an important Apostle after the crucifixion. It is also likely that he traveled extensively and preached for decades after the execution of Christ.

Nearly every source relates that Simon the Canaanite suffered death as a martyr. This being the case, it is safe to assume that the enemies of Christianity killed him for his faith. However, the where and when of his martyrdom are unknown.

## Matthias

Matthias was the 13th Apostle. The other Apostles chose him to replace Judas Iscariot (*Acts 1:15-27*).

Matthias had joined the movement early on. He was an active member of those Disciples working just below the level of the Apostles. However, he was not a unanimous choice to ascend the ladder to Apostle. The Apostles also considered a Disciple Joseph Barsabas, but settled upon Matthias.

After receiving his commission as Apostle, Matthias traveled to, and preached in, Ethiopia and the African interior. A story goes that Matthias ministered to cannibals in Africa. However, there is no absolute proof of this.

Later, Matthias traveled to Sebastopolis in present-day Turkey. Despite some reports that the Judeans beheaded Matthias in Jerusalem, the truth is that he died at Sebastopolis. We can be certain that Matthias did not die at Jerusalem because the source identifies Matthias as the "Bishop of Jerusalem." The truth is that James the Lesser was the Bishop of Jerusalem during the generation after Jesus suffered crucifixion. It is likely that the erroneous source confused James the Lesser with Matthias. Ancient sources also confuse Matthew and Matthias on a regular basis. This confusion occurred due to the similarities in spelling of the two names.

There is no evidence that Matthias actually suffered a martyr's death at Sebastopolis. However, there is no evidence to dispute it either.

# Conclusion

Politics has changed little in the two millennia since Jesus and his Apostles trod the earth together. We can see some of the same failings in politicians today as the politicians in the time of Jesus exhibited. The greed, the paranoia, the addiction to power, the willingness to form unholy alliances to overcome their enemies, are all just as common in present-day politics as they were in the time of Jesus.

Christians today understand that Jesus proclaimed a kingdom all could share after the fall of the present order. However, neither his enemies nor his followers could understand his message. They believed that he intended to overthrow Herod and establish himself as the King of Judea in their time. The Judean religious leaders did everything in their power to thwart Jesus and to maintain the status quo. When Jesus expired on the cross, they thought they had succeeded. However, they soon learned otherwise.

Neither could Rome prevent the Christians from pushing their message throughout the Empire. After centuries of persecuting Christians in the most brutal way, Rome finally succumbed and officially became a Christian state in 380 AD.

Of course, once the Christians became the most powerful religion in Rome, they used the resources of the vast Roman Empire, especially its trade connections, to spread the religious doctrine preached by Jesus across Europe, Asia, Africa and the entire globe, just as Jesus predicted they would. They still preach the message and still proclaim the kingdom today.

In retrospect, the trial and crucifixion of Jesus was unnecessary and counterproductive for both the Judeans and the Romans. The proof of this is that instead of silencing the Christian doctrine, the crucifixion spread it across the world. Not only did the crucifixion cause it to spread, the killing of Jesus caused it to spread with great speed. Secular leaders of today who use violence to counter doctrines they do not like could learn from the example of the murder of Jesus.

# Bibliography

Birks, H. A., *Studies in the life and character of St. Peter*, Hodder and Stoughton (1887)

Bryant, T. Alton, editor, *The New Compact Bible Dictionary*, Zondervan Publishing Company (1967).

Cheyne, Thomas Kelly and J. Sutherland Black, editors, *Encyclopaedia Biblica: A Critical Dictionary of the Literary, Political and Religion History, the Archeology, Geography and Natural History of the Bible*, (1899).

France, R. T., *The Gospel of Matthew (New International Commentary on the New Testament)*, Wm. B. Eerdmans Publishing Co (2007)

Graetz, Heinrich *History of the Jews*, Randolph Parrish, Editor, Wipf and Stock Publishers, (2012)

Josephus Flavius, *Jewish Antiquities*, republished, Acheron Press, (2012)

Kasher, Aryeh, *King Herod: A Persecuted Persecutor: A Case Study in Psychohistory and Psychobiography*, Walter de Gruyter, (2007)

*King James Version of the Bible*, (Public Domain)

# About the Author

CL Gammon has had a life-long fascination with history and writing. This fascination has led to his becoming an award-winning historian and an internationally known bestselling author. Scholars, educators and journalists recognize Gammon, who studied Political Science at Tennessee Technological University, as an authority on American political history. Several universities, including the State University of New York and the University of Akron, have used his writings as course material. Gammon is the author of more than twenty books. He lives in Lafayette, Tennessee with his family.

# Other Books by CL Gammon

CL Gammon has many interests and while most of his books are non-fiction, he has written books in several genres. You can find them all at Amazon.com or ask for them at your favorite bookstore. Below is a list of his books separated by genre.

## Local History

*Hanging the Macon County Witch*

## General History

*Was Lucille Ball a Communist?*

*Nazi Mad Science I: High Altitude Experiments*

*The True Story of Axis Sally*

*The Great Mormon War of 1857-1858*

*Why Johnson Created the Warren Commission*

*The Great New Hampshire Primary Myth*

*The Story of the First Continental Congress*

*Why the Articles of Confederation Failed*

*The Preamble of the United States Constitution*

*Seven Candidates for President in 1972*

*Guns, Politics and Independence*

*The Philosophy of the Confederate Constitution*

*Alexander Hamilton's Plan for America*

*America's First Rules of War*

*America's Other Party: A Brief History of the Prohibition Party*

*Abraham Lincoln: Warrior in Chief*

*The Continental Congress: America's Forgotten Government*

*Hail to the Chief: The Presidency by the Numbers*

*Make Sure You are Right, then Go Ahead and other Essays*

## Crime Novel

*The Big Fire*

## Christian Novel

*Simon the Accuser: A Christian Novel*

## Sports

Bad Football Saturday's 50 Worst Teams Ever!

www.ingramcontent.com/pod-product-compliance
Lightning Source LLC
Chambersburg PA
CBHW060421290526
45791CB00002B/845